Remembering Cleveland

Ronald L. Burdick and Margaret L. Baughman

TURNER
PUBLISHING COMPANY

A three-masted schooner rests moored on the Cuyahoga River in the year 1900. The early machinery in view was used for unloading ore, transported across the Great Lakes to Cleveland from Upper Michigan.

Remembering Cleveland

Turner Publishing Company
www.turnerpublishing.com

Remembering Cleveland

Copyright © 2010 Turner Publishing Company

Library of Congress Control Number: 2010923502

ISBN: 978-1-59652-632-7

Printed in the United States of America

ISBN 978-1-68336-819-9 (pbk.)

CONTENTS

The Morgan residence, Newburgh township, at what is now Broadway and Aetna Road in Cleveland, 1850.

ACKNOWLEDGMENTS

This volume, *Remembering Cleveland,* is the result of the cooperation and efforts of many individuals, organizations, and corporations. It is with great thanks that we acknowledge in particular the valuable contribution of the following for their generous support:

The Cleveland Public Library
The Library of Congress

The writers would like to thank the following individuals at Cleveland Public Library for their valuable contribution and assistance in making this work possible:

Colleagues
Jean M. Collins, Librarian, Literature Department
Amy E. Dawson, Librarian, Catalog Department
Maureen T. Mullin, Librarian, Head, Business, Economics, and Labor

Photograph Collection Staff
Venechor Boyd
Neletha Chambers
Elmer F. Turner III

PREFACE

Cleveland has thousands of historic photographs that reside in archives, both locally and nationally. This book began with the observation that, while those photographs are of great interest to many, they are not easily accessible. During a time when Cleveland is looking ahead and evaluating its future course, many people are asking, How do we treat the past? These decisions affect every aspect of the city—architecture, public spaces, commerce, infrastructure—and these, in turn, affect the way that people live their lives. This book seeks to provide easy access to a valuable, objective look into the history of Cleveland.

The power of photographs is that they are less subjective than words in their treatment of history. Although the photographer can make subjective decisions regarding subject matter and how to capture and present it, photographs seldom interpret the past to the extent textual histories can. For this reason, photography is uniquely positioned to offer an original, untainted look at the past, allowing the viewer to learn for himself what the world was like a century or more ago.

This project represents countless hours of review and research. The researchers and writers have reviewed thousands of photographs in numerous archives. We greatly appreciate the generous assistance of the individuals and organizations listed in the acknowledgments of this work, without whom this project could not have been completed.

The goal in publishing this work is to provide broader access to this set of extraordinary photographs that seek to inspire, provide perspective, and evoke insight that might assist people who are responsible for determining Cleveland's future. In addition, the book seeks to preserve the past with adequate respect and reverence.

With the exception of touching up imperfections that have accrued with the passage of time and cropping where necessary, no changes have been made. The focus and clarity of many images are limited to the technology and the ability of the photographer at the time they were recorded.

The work is divided into eras. Beginning with some of the earliest known photographs of Cleveland, the first section records photographs from the city's earliest days. The second section spans the decades between 1870 and 1929, Cleveland's "golden era." Section Three moves from the Great Depression to the World War II and early postwar eras. The last section concludes with a brief look at images from recent times.

In each of these sections we have made an effort to capture various aspects of life through our selection of photographs. People, commerce, transportation, infrastructure, religious institutions, and educational institutions have been included to provide a broad perspective.

We encourage readers to reflect as they go walking in Cleveland, strolling through the city, its parks, and its neighborhoods. It is the publisher's hope that in utilizing this work, longtime residents will learn something new and that new residents will gain a perspective on where Cleveland has been, so that each can contribute to its future.

—*Todd Bottorff, Publisher*

McIlrath Tavern, circa 1850. The hostelry was built by Abner McIlrath in 1832 at the northwest corner of Euclid and Superior avenues in East Cleveland. It served as tavern, voting place, and as an informal community center for many years. Following McIlrath's death the business closed, and after many years of neglect the building was razed, in 1890.

VILLAGE TO CITY

(1850s–1869)

This is the earliest known photograph of the Ohio and Erie Canal in Cleveland, circa 1859. Built in 1832, the canal's usefulness was ending as railroads became the preferred means of transport. These buildings stood in the Flats, east of the Cuyahoga River. The high ground visible at rear is a residential area south and east of downtown Cleveland.

Civil War veterans gather on Public Square in front of the post office building. The veterans display their battle flags during the ceremony for mustering out of the regiment.

A view of the pavilion and catafalque for the coffin of President Abraham Lincoln. The hearse and six white horses used to move Lincoln's coffin from the railroad terminal to the square are visible to the right of the pavilion.

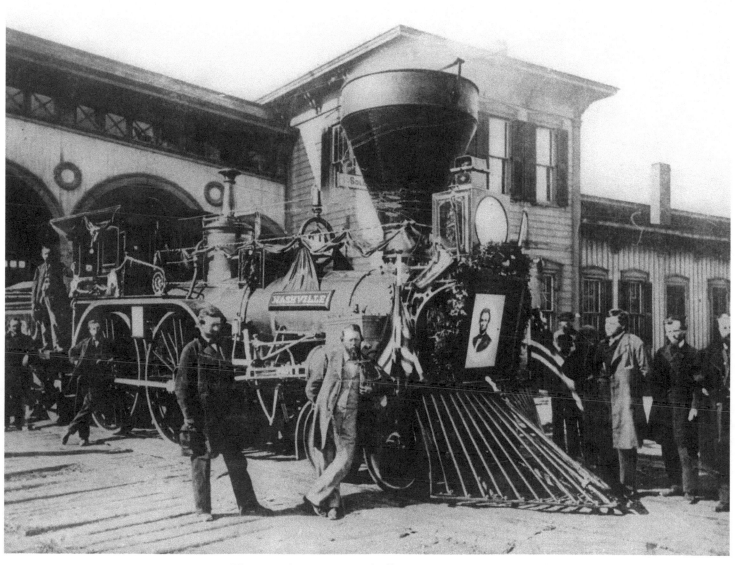

The steam locomotive *Nashville* at Union Station in 1865. The crew is waiting to take President Abraham Lincoln's body from Cleveland to Columbus.

Residence of John Blair at 802 Prospect Street, 1865. John Blair came to Cleveland in 1819 from Maryland with 3 dollars in his pockets. Within a few years he turned his speculation in pork into a large and prosperous produce and commission business, with a warehouse along the Cuyahoga River. Blair also served on the board of directors of the Commercial Bank of Lake Erie, and was elected Cleveland councilman in 1836.

Cleveland's "Golden Era"

(1870–1929)

The Jewish Orphan Asylum was dedicated on July 14, 1868, and opened with more than 80 residents. In 1888, the orphanage moved to this spacious building on Woodland Avenue, near East 55th Street. The building was leveled in 1929 to make way for new commercial and industrial development.

Looking across Public Square at the Lily Fountain in 1888. The tall building in the center background is the third building to serve as a courthouse for Cuyahoga County. The building to the right of the courthouse was the Hick Block, home to the Lyceum Theater for many years.

Uniformed war veterans march in the Washington Birthday parade past the house of D. W. Cross, located at 483 Euclid Avenue, in 1889. Cross was president of the Cleveland Steam Gauge Company.

Cleveland General Hospital, 1894. Operated by the Medical Department at the University of Wooster, the hospital's mission was to provide clinical training for medical students and a training school for nurses. It was located at Woodland Avenue near East 20th Street.

A piano is delivered to a residence on Rockwell Street circa 1880 by the B. Dreher's Sons Company, sales agent for Knabe and Haines Brothers Pianos and Organs, 371 and 373 Superior and 29 the Arcade.

Euclid Avenue, 1890. The tall building on the right is the Arcade. On the left is the Clarence Building at 122 Euclid. Theo Endean's portrait photography studio was located in room 62. At the time the business district still enjoyed mature stands of trees.

Pictured here are businesses along the north side of Euclid Avenue, just east of Public Square, in 1890.

A parade advances down Franklin Avenue, in the Ohio City neighborhood along the west side of the Cuyahoga River, in 1890. Ohio City and Cleveland had been competing communities until 1836, when the two villages merged to become the City of Cleveland.

The Pennsylvania Railroad depot at the corner of Euclid Avenue and East 55th Street (formerly Willson Avenue), in 1890.

Shown here is a portable voting booth at Public Square in 1890. Behind it are the Society for Savings building (left) and the Brainard building (right).

Public Square in 1896. The arch was a "Court of Honor" constructed as part of Cleveland's centennial celebration. Soldiers and Sailors Monument, honoring Cleveland's Civil War militia, is located to the right of the arch.

Female members of the Early Settlers Association pose for the photographer as streetcar no. 719 pulls into view.

Alexander Winton is seated at the tiller on this first demonstration of an automobile in Cleveland, captured here in front of the Winton Motor-Carriage Company on Berea Road in 1896. The Winton Company would produce automobiles until 1924.

The north side of Euclid Avenue between East 4th Street and Public Square. In view are the Arcade and the Halle Brothers Department Store. Electric streetcars began running in Cleveland in 1884.

Willie McKevitt sits at the controls of the first electric automobile built by Walter Baker in 1898, who founded the Baker Motor Vehicle Company in 1900, producing electric automobiles for only a brief time. The Baker Electric was slow, quiet, and popular with women, but was unable to compete with gasoline-powered automobiles being manufactured, because the batteries had to be recharged after 20 minutes of driving.

The Lake Erie lakefront, 1901. In the foreground is Lake View Park, Cleveland's first public park. Railroad tracks trace the shoreline.

Euclid Avenue at the intersection of East 14th Street in 1900. Visible is the Euclid Avenue Presbyterian Church, where today stands the Hanna Building.

The second Union Passenger Depot (constructed 1864–1866) in 1890. The first Union Passenger Depot, located on this site at the foot of Water (now East 9th) and Bank (now East 6th) streets along the lakefront, was a wood structure and was destroyed by fire in 1864. The second depot pictured here was a massive stone building 603 feet long and 180 feet wide. It was demolished in 1959.

Sheriff Street Market, opened in 1891, was the largest food market in Cleveland until 1924 with the construction of the new Westside Market building on West 25th Street in Ohio City. Owned and operated by Sheriff St. Market and Storage Company, the market building was located at the corner of Huron Road and Sheriff Street (now East 4th Street). It was a Cleveland landmark until a large portion of the building was destroyed by fire in 1930.

An interior view of the Winton Motor Carriage Company, sometime early in the twentieth century.

Soldiers and Sailors Monument in 1901. The monument was designed by Levi T. Scofield, and dedicated on July 4, 1894. It is located in the southeastern quadrant of Public Square and honors the men from Cleveland who served in the Civil War. The pillars surrounding the monument are swirled in black in this photograph in memory of President William McKinley, who had just been assassinated.

A winter view of Public Square in 1905. In the background is the New United States Court House, Customs House, and Post Office under construction.

The start of a race at the Glenville race track in 1903. Officials are Samuel Butler and Arthur Pardington. Cars and drivers (left to right) are: Paul Bainey's 4-cylinder French car, with Meyers driving; Kenigslow's two-cylinder auto, Walter Stone driving; Baker's (the Torpedo Kid) electric car, with Walter C. Baker driving and Fred H. White at the rear wheel; and the Olds "Go-Devil," with D. Wurgis driving.

Public Square circa 1900. Behind the Soldiers and Sailors Monument are the Cuyahoga and Williamson buildings. D. H. Burnham & Company designed the Cuyahoga, erected in 1893 as the first completely steel-framed building in Cleveland. The Williamson, the second building of that name to stand at the site, was built in 1899–1900. Both structures were leveled in 1982 to make way for the Standard Oil of Ohio building.

The U.S. Life Saving Service, 1905, with life-saving crew at drill. The service began in 1876 and was located at West Pier near the mouth of the Cuyahoga River. Eventually it would be merged with several other government agencies to form the U.S. Coast Guard.

Winter fun on Lake Erie. Ice boating was a popular sport early in the 1900s, made possible by the cold winters in Northeastern Ohio.

A banner on 6th Street at Superior Avenue announces the 1909 Industrial and Building Exposition, which was held at the end of 6th Street. The building on the left corner is the Plain Dealer's former headquarters.

Here in 1909, Clevelanders enjoy the "Great Aerial Swing" ride at Luna Park. The popular 35-acre park was developed by Fred Ingersoll, who specialized in amusement parks. Opening in 1905, it was located on Woodhill Road, near Woodland Avenue. Other attractions included a wooden track roller coaster, "Shoot the Chute" water ride, and a small replica of India's Taj Mahal.

Mounted police pose for a photograph in 1909 in front of the Central Armory, located near the north end of East 6th Street. The armory was built in 1893 by Cuyahoga County to house the Ohio National Guard and was also used to host large public events when not being used by the Guard. It was demolished during Urban Renewal in the 1960s.

Ice skaters enjoy the day at Rockefeller Park early in the 1900s.

Pictured here in front of Rockwell School on East 6th Street in 1908, President William Howard Taft tours Cleveland in an automobile.

A view of the western end of the Pennsylvania Railroad depot on Euclid Avenue at the corner of East 55th Street.

A wide view of the Detroit Superior Bridge. Built 1914–1918, it is a main artery connecting the east and west sides of Cleveland. The two-level bridge carried automobile and pedestrian traffic on the upper level and electric streetcars on the lower level. The central span is 592 feet long, rises 196 feet above the river, and is anchored by 12 concrete arches.

The Hollenden Hotel at the corner of Superior and East 6th Street circa 1900. The grandest hotel in Cleveland at the time it opened in 1885, the eight-story hotel featured electric lights and its dining room was a popular gathering spot for visiting dignitaries including United States presidents, local politicians, and the well-to-do of Cleveland.

Edward J. Weigel's butcher shop inside the Westside Market on West 25th Street, in the Ohio City neighborhood.

Passengers board a train at the Pennsylvania Depot in 1908.

Soldiers and Sailors Monument on Public Square. At left is Midland Bank in the Williamson Building, and at right is the May Company building, as it appeared in 1914 before two floors were added to the structure (in 1931). The May building remains, but the Williamson Building was razed in 1982 to make room for the new Standard Oil of Ohio office building.

Glenn Curtiss in 1910 prepares to take off from Euclid Beach Park for a flight of 60 miles to Cedar Point, Sandusky, Ohio.

A sightseeing automobile filled with visitors departs Public Square in 1910 for a tour of the Euclid-Wade & Gordon parks and boulevard.

In October 1910, spectators climb onto parked streetcars in Public Square for a view of the Cuyahoga County Centennial Parade.

Street cleaners work along Franklin Hill in the Ohio City neighborhood about 1910.

The lakefront, 1911. Seen from the breakwater, in front of the railroad tracks is the Cleveland Yacht Club (with the twin-gabled roof) sitting over Lake Erie at the foot of East 9th Street. Behind the yacht club and up the hill is the U.S. Marine Hospital and to the left is Lakeside Hospital. In the middle ground is a dumping platform.

Grocery shopping, 1911-style.

Euclid Avenue at E. 17th Street. Spanish-American War veterans march on the far side of Euclid Avenue while the Knights of St. John march on the near side in the opposite direction.

Established in 1894, the Cleveland Trust Bank was an important banking institution. The bank moved into this imposing building in 1907. The building features a large Tiffany-glass rotunda 85 feet above the first floor. Currently being remodeled to serve county government offices, the building's future seems bright.

The youth of one Cleveland neighborhood pose for the photographer in 1911.

John D. and Laura Rockefeller debark a train at the Nickel Plate Station in Cleveland about 1912. Rockefeller built the Standard Oil Company, which he founded in Cleveland, into the largest oil-refining company in the world. His first oil refinery was located in the Flats area south of the city.

Horse-drawn vehicles, automobiles, streetcars, and pedestrians negotiate Euclid Avenue in 1912.

A busy street corner in downtown Cleveland in 1912, opposite Public Square. In view at center, next door to the May Company, the Crow & Whitmarsh Company sold dry goods and notions.

The Union Depot tracks and covered bridge in 1914. By the 1890s it had become difficult for Union Depot to handle the volume of train traffic coming into Cleveland. After Terminal Tower was built in 1927, Union Depot lost most of its business. The depot closed in 1953 and was demolished in 1959.

A bird's-eye view from East 6th Street. In 1914, Euclid Avenue was an important commercial, shopping, and entertainment center.

Euclid Avenue in 1915. Once known as Doan's Corners, Euclid Avenue between East 105th and 107th streets was considered Cleveland's second downtown.

A view of the Detroit-Superior Bridge in 1915. The lake freighter *Christopher* in the Cuyahoga River is being moved by tugs. Fairchild's Flour Mill stands on the east bank.

An American tank on display at Public Square serves as a booth for the sale of war bonds to support the American Expeditionary Forces in World War I.

A crowd of Clevelanders gathers at the Union Terminal for the send-off of the 5th Regiment of the Ohio National Guard, to fight the Axis Forces in Europe in World War I.

In 1918, a World War I war bonds tent on the northwest quadrant of Public Square is open for business, helping to win the war by funding the war effort.

Pictured here are some of the Clevelanders who gathered on Public Square November 11, 1918, to celebrate the Armistice ending World War I.

Mouth of the Cuyahoga River and the Flats area. A passenger steamboat is docked along the west bank of the river in front of the Cleveland Electric Illuminating Company's former powerhouse. At right-center is Whiskey Island, a peninsula formed by the old river bed and new river channel, and named for an early distillery, which operated on the site.

Huron Road, 1921. The triangle-shaped Osborn Block stands at the intersection of Huron Road and Prospect Avenue at East 9th Street.

Shoppers examine merchandise in vendors' stalls outside the Westside Market on West 25th Street. Opened in 1924, the market is still in operation, and has become an important tourist attraction for the city, besides serving as the city's largest market for meat, poultry, fish, ethnic foods, fresh produce, fresh cut flowers, and other desired delicacies.

These retail and office buildings occupied the south side of Public Square before their demolition for the building of the Cleveland Union Terminal and Terminal Tower Complex.

Edgewater Park, 1922. Located along Lake Erie west of downtown, the park was purchased in 1894 by the City of Cleveland, from Jacob B. Perkins, Cleveland industrialist. Recreational facilities included bathhouses, a pavilion, baseball diamonds, and picnic and playground areas. It also held the Edgewater Yacht Club and the Edgewater Lagoon.

A view of the East 9th Street lagoon with several small private pleasure boats tied up at the docks. The Cleveland Boat Club building is visible at left.

Children in costume parade down Euclid Avenue around 1920, in the annual Playground Parade, a highlight of Cleveland's summer recreation program.

The western end of Euclid Avenue at Public Square circa 1920. At left is the Euclid Avenue entrance to the Midland Bank in the Williamson Building, and at right is Bailey's Department Store and the western corner of the May Company building.

A policeman directs traffic at the northwest corner of Euclid Avenue and East 107th Street in 1922.

Early arrivals to the Republican National Convention, held in Cleveland in 1924, receive stuffed elephants as welcoming gifts. The women are delegates representing the Woman's Republican Club of Massachusetts and of New York.

Republican delegates fill Cleveland's new Public Hall, which opened in 1922 with seating for 13,000. Public Hall still provides space for large meetings and conventions in the city.

Barbers from George A. Myers barbershop in the Hollenden Hotel line up for a group portrait. The barbershop rivaled the hotel's bar as a center for political activity, and was also one of the most modern in the nation, with porcelain fixtures, individual wash basins, sterilizers, and humidors. The writer Elbert Hubbard described the shop as "the best barber shop in America," and Myers boasted of shaving or barbering eight presidents, several congressmen, and other luminaries such as Mark Twain, Lloyd George, and Marshall Foch.

A 1925 view of Public Square and the Soldiers and Sailors Monument, from the vantage point of the Williamson Building. Left of the Old Stone Church (First Presbyterian) is the 1915 Illuminating Building, and to the right of the church, across Ontario Street, is the Society for Savings Building constructed in 1889-90.

Noted photographer Margaret Bourke-White takes up a precarious position on the roof of an office building across Superior Avenue from the recently opened Main Building of the Cleveland Public Library. To the right of the library is the old Plain Dealer building, now the site of the Library's Louis Stokes Wing. The taller building behind the Plain Dealer building houses the Federal Reserve Bank of Cleveland.

The Standard Brewing Company's horse-drawn beer wagon plies the streets of Cleveland, circa 1910.

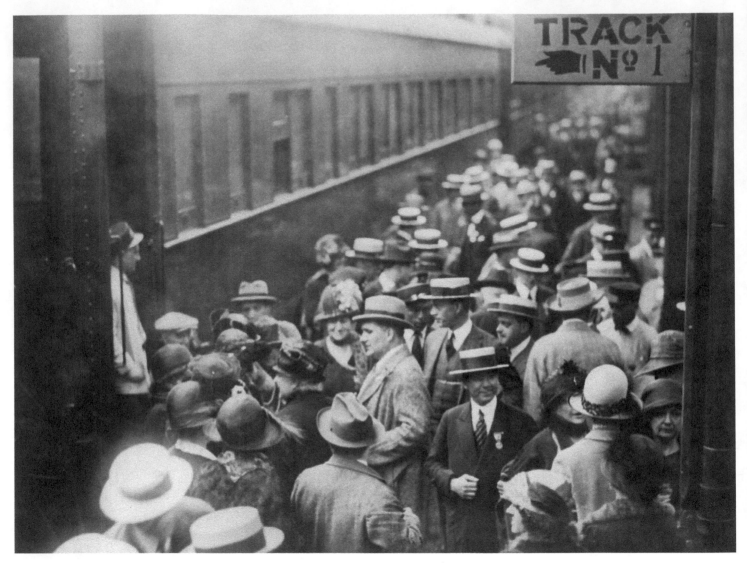

Massachusetts delegates arrive in Cleveland for the Republican National Convention in 1924.

A view of East 105th Street from about 100 feet south of Massie Avenue in 1928. The busy street is shared by automobiles and electric streetcars.

An airplane sits parked at the terminal at newly opened Cleveland Hopkins Airport in 1928. Ford Commercial Air Lines inaugurated daily flights between Cleveland and Detroit in airplanes like the one pictured here. The flight between the cities took one hour and twenty minutes to complete.

A large crowd gathers to watch fire fighters work at putting out the fire at the Cleveland Clinic building at East 93rd Street on May 15, 1929. A storage room containing X-ray film caught fire, creating a lethal gas that killed 124 persons, including 9 doctors. An electric light bulb left on and located too close to the X-ray film was determined to be the cause of the fire.

Lexington Avenue at East 66th Street. This aerial view was taken during the World Series games of October 1920. League Park, a Cleveland landmark, was formerly known as Cleveland Baseball Park.

Spectators view the United States Navy's dirigible airship USS *Los Angles* at its mooring at National Air Races at the Cleveland Airport in 1929. One of the thrills of the show in 1929 was the transfer of Lieutenant Bolster from *Los Angles* to a Vought biplane moored on the underside of the dirigible.

An anxious mother and small child navigate their way through a crowd of shoppers selecting fresh produce from stands set up on the sidewalk along Lorain Avenue outside the Westside Market in 1927.

A Cleveland Public Library book caravan visits Sowinski School at Sowinski Avenue near East 79th Street.

The head of one of the heroic pieces of sculpture that will grace the new Lorain-Carnegie high-level span is being lowered into place in 1932. These pylons (there are four, each having figures facing east and west) rise 45 feet above the bridge sidewalk.

THE GREAT DEPRESSION AND WORLD WAR II

(1930–1949)

The freighter *G. A. Tomlinson* is towed on the Cuyahoga River through the Flats in 1936.

Thousands of Cleveland spectators view uniformed policemen as they proceed west on Euclid Avenue toward Public Square on August 1, 1933. This was Cleveland's first National Recovery Act parade.

An aerial view of the Cleveland Municipal Stadium. Spectators fill the walkways leading into the stadium to watch a Cleveland Indians' game in 1935. The stadium was completed in 1931.

The lakefront takes on the appearance of a frozen wonderland in this photograph taken in December 1938. Captain W. E. Crapo of the United States Coast Guard and the station's mascot Rex look out over Lake Erie.

The Cleveland Cultural Gardens were established in 1926 to represent Cleveland's cultural diversity. Representing people of different ethnic nationalities who came to live and work in Cleveland, the individual gardens pay tribute to the best artists, scientists, and thinkers with sculpture, fountains, and landscaping. Work is in progress here in 1936.

A crowd of Clevelanders welcomes President Franklin Delano Roosevelt (riding in the lead car) to the city in 1936. President Roosevelt was in Cleveland to attend the Great Lakes Exposition.

A view of the Great Lakes Exposition of 1936 and 1937 from above. Approximately 7 million visitors had spent nearly $70 million by the end of the second year.

The Bug was a popular ride at Euclid Beach Park in 1937. Incorporated in 1894, the amusement park was modeled after New York's Coney Island. It would entertain Clevelanders for nearly 75 years.

A view of the midway and crowd at the Cleveland Exposition along the lakeshore north of the city on September 8, 1936. The crowd reportedly surpassed 83,000 people on that particular day.

The Cleveland skyline from Edgewater Park. Choppy waves on Lake Erie suggest that Cleveland was experiencing a blustery day.

The double-deck Detroit-Superior Bridge (now Veterans Memorial Bridge) viewed from the Cuyahoga River, 1936. Completed in 1918, when it opened it was the largest double-deck bridge in the world. The upper deck of the bridge carried automobile and pedestrian traffic; the lower deck carried streetcar traffic from the west side into the Cleveland Terminal.

Model boat enthusiasts launch their sailboats in the Cleveland Board of Education's model boat regatta at the Rockefeller Park pond in 1939.

Terminal Tower completed in 1929 overlooks construction of Cleveland's new Union Terminal. The railroad station when completed in 1930 was the largest in the nation, featuring a large portico with a high vaulted ornamental plaster ceiling and skylight. The completed terminal clerestory (skylight) is visible in front of the rising girders of the Prospect buildings (Midland, Republic, and Guildhall buildings) to the right of Terminal Tower.

In 1944, the sad aftermath of the East Ohio Gas Company explosion and fire included recovery of burned bodies from the ruins of buildings. Pictured is the search at the gas company's meter house.

The original terminal at Cleveland
Hopkins Municipal (now
Cleveland Hopkins International)
Airport. The airport had opened
in 1925 on 1,040 acres of land on
the southern edge of the city, with
the terminal following in 1929.

Shoppers throng the sidewalks along the 200 block of Euclid Avenue in 1941. The street is crowded with streetcars, automobiles, and buses.

In 1941, in the northwest quadrant of Public Square, members of the Cleveland fire department demonstrate how to handle incendiary bombs. The Illuminating Building and the Old Stone Church are visible in the background.

Reservists in 1942 move through the crowd at Public Square to watch the drawing for call-up for active duty in World War II.

A float in the July 4th parade, 1941, at the Cleveland Municipal Stadium.

Colonel William C. McCally, chief of surgery and commanding officer of Cleveland's Lakeside Hospital Unit, holds a nurses inspection on the grounds of the Royal Melbourne Hospital in Australia, shortly after the unit arrived there in 1942.

The *Spirit of Cleveland,* a four-engine Flying Fortress purchased with proceeds from the "Buy a Bomber for MacArthur" campaign. Mrs. Frank J. Lausche, wife of the mayor of Cleveland, christens the plane while a small crowd watches on July 2, 1942.

Dry dock of the American Shipbuilding Company, founded in 1899 and a leading designer and builder of Great Lakes vessels. The largest shipbuilder on the Great Lakes by 1952, labor conflicts and a decline in Great Lakes shipping caused the company to cease operations in northeast Ohio in 1983.

The War Service Center building at its dedication in August 1942, with war equipment on loan for the dedication celebration. The building was located on the northwest quadrant of Public Square.

The War Service Center included a small playground area for children. In this view from 1943, children could enjoy the teeter-totter, swings, and other equipment.

Rockefeller Park Lagoon, 1943.

The White Motor Company half-track combat vehicle assembly line, 1941.

Cleveland celebrates victory over Japan and the end of World War II with a parade down Euclid
Avenue near 9th Street, August 15, 1945.

Euclid Avenue, 1946. In this view east, the former Higbee Company building is visible on the left. It was occupied by the Navy during and after World War II. In 1949 the building became the Lindner-Davis department store.

On September 5, 1950, a crowd gathers in front of the Public Square entrance of Terminal Tower to send United States Marines off to duty in the Korean War.

The Cleveland Browns and the San Francisco 49ers battle it out on December 1, 1949, in the Cleveland Municipal Stadium. This was the last year that both teams played as members of the All-American Football Conference. In 1950 the league folded and both teams became members of the National Football League.

After a snowstorm in November 1949, Arthur Godfrey's talent scouts may find the pickings slim here at Playhouse Square.

Holiday shoppers do not seem bothered by the falling snow in this photograph of Euclid Avenue just east of 4th Street.

An aerial view of Cleveland circa 1950, facing south. The Terminal Tower dominates the city skyline.

Dealing with Adversity

(1950–1965)

A Lake Erie freighter maneuvers up the Cuyahoga River, circa 1960. The Flats (flood plain) and the Cleveland skyline are visible in the right foreground and background.

A view of Euclid Avenue at East 105th Street circa 1956. Buses have replaced streetcars, which ended service in January 1954. Playing at the theater is *Written on the Wind,* starring Rock Hudson and Lauren Bacall.

Severance Hall, in University Circle, home of the world-renowned Cleveland Orchestra, was completed in 1931.

The Cleveland Museum of Art, 1959. At the back of the photograph, between the two middle ionic columns, is the *Thinker,* a Rodin sculpture. In the forefront is the *Fountain of the Waters.*

Thousands of Clevelanders gather in front of the Terminal Tower to welcome Dwight D. Eisenhower to Cleveland.

A band marches past Soldiers and Sailors Monument on Euclid Avenue in a parade commemorating the sesquicentennial of the Battle of Lake Erie during the War of 1812.

The interior of the Arcade, from the Superior Avenue entrance, circa 1960. Built in 1890 and opened on Memorial Day, it cost $867,000 to complete. The structure is internationally known and has been compared to the Galleria Vittorio En Arcade in Milan, Italy. The Arcade is 300 feet long, 4 levels high, and is crowned with a glass-domed ceiling rising about 100 feet above the main floor.

A view of the gardens at the Samuel Mather house on Euclid Avenue in 1965. This was one of the last remnants of Euclid Avenue's "Millionaires' Row" to survive. The gardens were later paved over and used as a driving school for the Cleveland Automobile Association.

NOTES ON THE PHOTOGRAPHS

These notes, listed by page number, attempt to include all aspects known of the photographs. Each of the photographs is identified by the page number, a title or description, photographer and collection, archive, and call or box number when applicable. Although every attempt was made to collect all data, in some cases complete data may have been unavailable due to the age and condition of some of the photographs and records.